I0866842

SECURE IN THE STORM

Scriptures for Your Time of Need

Julie Yarbrough

Abingdon Press
Nashville

SECURE IN THE STORM:
SCRIPTURES FOR YOUR TIME OF NEED

This book is printed on acid-free paper.
ISBN 978-1-4267-6894-1

13 14 15 16 17 18 19 20 21 22—10 9 8 7 6 5 4 3 2 1

MANUFACTURED IN THE UNITED STATES OF AMERICA

Whatever your storm
may be, this pocket-sized
book is a collection of verses
offering comfort, support,
and encouragement.

Julie

Contents

Introduction 7

1. Assurance 13

2. Comfort 23

3. Encouragement 29

4. Faith 43

5. Hope 49

6. Love 55

7. Peace 61

Introduction

My husband, Leighton Farrell, was Senior Minister at Highland Park United Methodist Church in Dallas, Texas, for twenty-three years. In the early 1980s, a church member who was also a dear friend of my husband became terminally ill. His name was Dee. To offer hope and encouragement to Dee in the last months of his life, Leighton shared with him forty-seven Bible verses that were especially meaningful to him. His collection of Scripture, entitled *Secure in the Storm*, was later printed and offered to many in need of spiritual support, especially at times of illness and death. Now an expanded collection is available in this format to provide the same kind of spiritual support to anyone experiencing a time of need.

I use *Secure in the Storm* every day as part of my personal devotion time. These passages from God's Word have been a stronghold in my life, especially since the death of my beloved husband in 2004. I discern within each well-chosen verse the enduring quality of biblical faith that sustained Leighton's spiritual journey and that continues to inspire my own.

Perhaps you have come face-to-face with death as I have. Or perhaps you have experienced some other kind of loss or time of trial, whether financial, physical, relational, or otherwise. Whatever your storm may be, this pocket-sized book is a collection of verses offering comfort, support, and encouragement. It is my prayer that these promises of the Bible will strengthen you and sustain you in the steadfast love and faithfulness of God on your journey through life, as they have for me. Through the power of the Holy Spirit at work in our lives in ways unknown and unseen to us, may we find comfort and hope and the assurance that whatever storm we are facing, we are secure in the loving embrace of God.

Julie Yarbrough

Your word is a lamp to my feet
and a light to my path.
Psalm 119:105

ASSURANCE

1

ASSURANCE

Know therefore that the Lord your God is God; he is the faithful God, keeping his covenant of love to a thousand generations of those who love him and keep his commands.

Deuteronomy 7:9 NIV

"The eternal God is your refuge,
and underneath are the everlasting arms."

Deuteronomy 33:27 NIV

"I will be with you; I will not fail you or forsake you."

Joshua 1:5

"But those who suffer he delivers in their suffering;
he speaks to them in their affliction."

Job 36:15 NIV

In peace I will both lie down and sleep;
for thou alone, O LORD, makest me dwell in safety.

Psalm 4:8 RSV

And those who know your name put their trust in you,
for you, O LORD, have not forsaken those who seek you.

Psalm 9:10

This God—his way is perfect;
the promise of the LORD proves true;
he is a shield for all who take refuge in him.

Psalm 18:30

You have turned my mourning into dancing;
you have taken off my sackcloth
and clothed me with joy,
so that my soul may praise you and not be silent.
O LORD my God, I will give thanks to you forever.

Psalm 30:11-12

When the righteous cry for help, the LORD hears,
and rescues them from all their troubles.
The LORD is near to the brokenhearted,
and saves the crushed in spirit.

Many are the afflictions of the righteous,
    but the LORD rescues them from them all.
        Psalm 34:17-19

Cast your cares on the LORD
    and he will sustain you;
he will never let
    the righteous fall.
        Psalm 55:22 NIV 1984

One thing God has spoken,
    two things have I heard:
that you, O God, are strong,
    and that you, O Lord, are loving.
        Psalm 62:11-12 NIV 1984

A father to the fatherless, a defender of widows,
    is God in his holy dwelling.
        Psalm 68:5 NIV

Love and faithfulness meet together;
    righteousness and peace kiss each other.
Faithfulness springs forth from the earth,
    and righteousness looks down from heaven.
        Psalm 85:10-11 NIV

Light dawns for the righteous,
   and joy for the upright in heart.
      Psalm 97:11

Precious in the sight of the LORD
   is the death of his faithful ones.
      Psalm 116:15

The LORD lifts up those who are bowed down; . . .
   he upholds the widow and the fatherless.
      Psalm 146:8-9 ESV

He heals the brokenhearted,
   and binds up their wounds.
      Psalm 147:3

For everything there is a season, and a time for every matter under heaven:

   a time to be born, and a time to die.
      Ecclesiastes 3:1-2

He gives power to the faint,
   and strengthens the powerless.
      Isaiah 40:29

I will turn their mourning into joy,
    I will comfort them, and give them gladness for sorrow.

Jeremiah 31:13b

I will satisfy the weary,
    and all who are faint I will replenish.

Jeremiah 31:25

"Come to me, all you that are weary and are carrying heavy burdens, and I will give you rest. Take my yoke upon you, and learn from me; for I am gentle and humble in heart, and you will find rest for your souls. For my yoke is easy, and my burden is light."

Matthew 11:28-30

"I am the resurrection and the life; he who believes in me, though he die, yet shall he live, and whoever lives and believes in me shall never die."

John 11:25-26 RSV

"If you abide in me, and my words abide in you, ask for whatever you wish, and it will be done for you."

John 15:7

"Now is your time of grief, but I will see you again and you will rejoice, and no one will take away your joy."

John 16:22 NIV

We know that in everything God works for good with those who love him, who are called according to his purpose.

Romans 8:28 RSV

Who shall separate us from the love of Christ? Shall tribulation, or distress, or persecution, or famine, or nakedness, or peril, or sword? As it is written,

> "For thy sake we are being killed all the day long;
> we are regarded as sheep to be slaughtered."

No, in all these things we are more than conquerors through him who loved us. For I am sure that neither death, nor life, nor angels, nor principalities, nor things present, nor things to come, nor powers, nor height, nor depth, nor anything else in all creation, will be able to separate us from the love of God in Christ Jesus our Lord.

Romans 8:35-39 RSV

No testing has overtaken you that is not common to everyone. God is faithful, and he will not let you be tested beyond your strength, but with the testing he will also provide the way out so that you may be able to endure it.

1 Corinthians 10:13

"My grace is sufficient for you, for power is made perfect in weakness."

2 Corinthians 12:9a

Draw near to God, and he will draw near to you.

James 4:8

And after you have suffered for a little while, the God of all grace, who has called you to his eternal glory in Christ, will himself restore, support, strengthen, and establish you.

1 Peter 5:10-11

"[God] will wipe every tear from their eyes.
Death will be no more;
mourning and crying and pain will be no more."

Revelation 21:4

COMFORT

2

COMFORT

"It is the Lord who goes before you; he will be with you, he will not fail you or forsake you; do not fear or be dismayed."

Deuteronomy 31:8 RSV

"As for me, I would seek God,
and to God I would commit my cause.
He does great things and unsearchable,
marvellous things without number . . .
he sets on high those who are lowly,
and those who mourn are lifted to safety."

Job 5:8-9, 11

I bless the Lord who gives me counsel;
in the night also my heart instructs me.
I keep the Lord always before me;
because he is at my right hand, I shall not be moved.

Psalm 16:7-8

The LORD is my shepherd, I shall not want;
    he makes me lie down in green pastures.
He leads me beside still waters;
    he restores my soul.
He leads me in paths of righteousness
    for his name's sake.

Even though I walk through the valley of the shadow of death,
    I fear no evil;
for thou art with me;
    thy rod and thy staff,
    they comfort me.

Thou preparest a table before me
    in the presence of my enemies;
thou anointest my head with oil,
    my cup overflows.
Surely goodness and mercy shall follow me
    all the days of my life;
and I shall dwell in the house of the LORD
    for ever.

Psalm 23 RSV

Be gracious to me, O LORD, for I am in distress;
    my eye wastes away from grief,
    my soul and body also.

Psalm 31:9

God is our refuge and strength,
a very present help in trouble.
Therefore we will not fear, though the earth should change,
though the mountains shake in the heart of the sea;
though its waters roar and foam,
though the mountains tremble with its tumult.

Psalm 46:1-3

But I am lowly and in pain;
let your salvation, O God, protect me.

Psalm 69:29

You who have done great things,
O God, who is like you?
You who have made me see many troubles and calamities
will revive me again;
from the depths of the earth
you will bring me up again.
You will increase my honor,
and comfort me once again.

Psalm 71:19b-21

My soul melts away for sorrow;
strengthen me according to your word.

Psalm 119:28

This is my comfort in my distress,
    that your promise gives me life.
        Psalm 119:50

For the LORD has comforted his people,
    and will have compassion on his suffering ones.
        Isaiah 49:13b

"Blessed are those who mourn, for they will be comforted."

Matthew 5:4

"Let not your hearts be troubled; believe in God, believe also in me. In my Father's house are many rooms; if it were not so, would I have told you that I go to prepare a place for you? And when I go and prepare a place for you, I will come again and will take you to myself, that where I am you may be also."

John 14:1-3 RSV

Praise be to the God and Father of our Lord Jesus Christ, the Father of compassion and the God of all comfort, who comforts us in all our troubles, so that we can comfort those in any trouble with the comfort we ourselves have received from God.

2 Corinthians 1:3-4 NIV

ENCOURAGEMENT

3

ENCOURAGEMENT

"My presence will go with you, and I will give you rest."

Exodus 33:14

Now choose life, so that you and your children may live and that you may love the LORD your God, listen to his voice, and hold fast to him. For the LORD is your life.

Deuteronomy 30:19-20 NIV

"Be strong and of good courage, do not fear or be in dread…for it is the LORD your God who goes with you; he will not fail you or forsake you."

Deuteronomy 31:6 RSV

"Have I not commanded you? Be strong and of good courage; be not frightened, neither be dismayed; for the LORD your God is with you wherever you go."

Joshua 1:9 RSV

Indeed, you are my lamp, O Lord,
the Lord lightens my darkness.
2 Samuel 22:29

Seek the Lord and his strength,
seek his presence continually.
1 Chronicles 16:11

You make known to me the path of life;
in your presence there is fullness of joy.
Psalm 16:11 ESV

Make me to know your ways, O Lord;
teach me your paths.
Psalm 25:4

The Lord is my light and my salvation;
whom shall I fear?
The Lord is the stronghold of my life;
of whom shall I be afraid?
Psalm 27:1

I believe that I shall see the goodness of the LORD
in the land of the living.
Wait for the LORD;
be strong, and let your heart take courage;
wait for the LORD!

Psalm 27:13-14

Weeping may linger for the night,
but joy comes with the morning.

Psalm 30:5b

I will instruct you and teach you the way you should go;
I will counsel you with my eye upon you.

Psalm 32:8

I sought the LORD, and he answered me,
and delivered me from all my fears.

Psalm 34:4

For with you is the fountain of life;
in your light we see light.

Psalm 36:9

Our steps are made firm by the LORD,
when he delights in our way;
though we stumble, we shall not fall headlong,
for the LORD holds us by the hand.
Psalm 37:23-24

"Be still, and know that I am God!"
Psalm 46:10

When I am afraid,
I will trust in you.
In God, whose word I praise,
in God I trust; I will not be afraid.
What can mortal man do to me?
Psalm 56:3-4 NIV 1984

Nevertheless I am continually with you;
you hold my right hand.
You guide me with your counsel,
and afterward you will receive me with honor.
Psalm 73:23-24

Seek the LORD and his strength;
seek his presence continually.
Psalm 105:4

Gracious is the Lord, and righteous;
    our God is merciful.
The Lord protects the simple;
    when I was brought low, he saved me.
Return, O my soul, to your rest,
    for the Lord has dealt bountifully with you.

Psalm 116:5-7

The people walking in darkness
    have seen a great light;
on those living in the land of the shadow of death
    a light has dawned.

Isaiah 9:2 NIV 1984

And when you turn to the right or when you turn to the left, your ears shall hear a word behind you, saying, "This is the way; walk in it."

Isaiah 30:21

Even youths will faint and be weary,
    and the young will fall exhausted;
but those who wait for the Lord shall renew their strength,
    they shall mount up with wings like eagles,
they shall run and not be weary,
    they shall walk and not faint.

Isaiah 40:30-31

Fear not, for I am with you,
be not dismayed, for I am your God;
I will strengthen you, I will help you,
I will uphold you with my victorious right hand.
Isaiah 41:10 RSV

For I, the Lord your God,
hold your right hand;
it is I who say to you, "Do not fear,
I will help you."
Isaiah 41:13

For my thoughts are not your thoughts,
nor are your ways my ways, says the Lord.
For as the heavens are higher than the earth,
so are my ways higher than your ways
and my thoughts than your thoughts.
Isaiah 55:8-9

The Lord will be your everlasting light,
and your God will be your glory.
Isaiah 60:19 NIV

The Spirit of the Lord God is upon me,
Because the Lord has anointed me
To bring good news to the afflicted;
He has sent me to bind up the brokenhearted…
To comfort all who mourn…
Giving them a garland instead of ashes,
The oil of gladness instead of mourning,
The mantle of praise instead of a spirit of fainting.
So they will be called oaks of righteousness,
The planting of the Lord, that He may be glorified.

Isaiah 61:1-3 NASB

When you search for me, you will find me; if you seek me with all your heart.

Jeremiah 29:13

"Therefore do not worry about tomorrow, for tomorrow will worry about itself. Each day has enough trouble of its own."

Matthew 6:34 NIV

"Ask, and it will be given you; search, and you will find; knock, and the door will be opened for you. For everyone who asks receives, and everyone who searches finds, and for everyone who knocks, the door will be opened.

Matthew 7:7-8

We rejoice in our sufferings, knowing that suffering produces endurance, and endurance produces character, and character produces hope.

Romans 5:3-4 RSV

To set the mind on the flesh is death, but to set the mind on the Spirit is life and peace.

Romans 8:6

Do not conform any longer to the pattern of this world, but be transformed by the renewing of your mind. Then you will be able to test and approve what God's will is—his good, pleasing and perfect will.

Romans 12:2 NIV

Rejoice in hope, be patient in suffering, persevere in prayer.

Romans 12:12

We do not live to ourselves, and we do not die to ourselves. If we live, we live to the Lord, and if we die, we die to the Lord; so then, whether we live or whether we die, we are the Lord's.

Romans 14:7-8

We are hard pressed on every side, but not crushed; perplexed, but not in despair; persecuted, but not abandoned; struck down, but not destroyed.

2 Corinthians 4:8-9 NIV

So we do not lose heart. Even though our outer nature is wasting away, our inner nature is being renewed day by day. For this slight momentary affliction is preparing us for an eternal weight of glory beyond all measure, because we look not at what can be seen but at what cannot be seen; for what can be seen is temporary, but what cannot be seen is eternal.

2 Corinthians 4:16-18

The fruit of the Spirit is love, joy, peace, patience, kindness, generosity, faithfulness, gentleness, and self-control.

Galatians 5:22-23

If we live by the Spirit, let us also be guided by the Spirit.

Galatians 5:25

Finally, be strong in the Lord and in the strength of his power.

Ephesians 6:10

But this one thing I do: forgetting what lies behind and straining forward to what lies ahead, I press on toward the goal for the prize of the heavenly call of God in Christ Jesus.

Philippians 3:13-14

I can do all things through him who strengthens me.

Philippians 4:13

Now may our Lord Jesus Christ himself and God our Father, who loved us and by his grace gave us eternal encouragement and good hope, encourage your hearts and strengthen you in every good deed and word.

2 Thessalonians 2:16-17 NIV

The widow who is really in need and left all alone puts her hope in God and continues night and day to pray and to ask God for help.

1 Timothy 5:5 NIV

For God has not given us a spirit of fear, but of power and of love and of a sound mind.

2 Timothy 1:7 NKJV

Blessed is the one who perseveres under trial because, having stood the test, that person will receive the crown of life that the Lord has promised to those who love him.

James 1:12 NIV

Humble yourselves, therefore, under God's mighty hand, that he may lift you up in due time. Cast all your anxiety on him because he cares for you.

1 Peter 5:6-7 NIV

FAITH

4

FAITH

The Lord is my strength and my shield;
    in him my heart trusts.
Psalm 28:7

But I trust in you, O Lord;
    I say "You are my God."
Psalm 31:14

I waited patiently for the Lord;
    he inclined to me and heard my cry.
He drew me up from the desolate pit,
    out of the miry bog,
and set my feet upon a rock,
    making my steps secure.
He put a new song in my mouth,
    a song of praise to our God.
Many will see and fear,
    and put their trust in the Lord.
Psalm 40:1-3

But my eyes are turned toward you, O God, my LORD;
in you I seek refuge; do not leave me defenseless.
Psalm 141:8

Trust in the LORD with all your heart,
and do not rely on your own insight.
In all your ways acknowledge him,
and he will make straight your paths.
Proverbs 3:5-6

The human mind plans the way,
but the LORD directs the steps.
Proverbs 16:9

Those of steadfast mind you keep in peace—
in peace because they trust in you.
Isaiah 26:3

Trust in the LORD forever,
for in the LORD GOD
you have an everlasting rock.
Isaiah 26:4

In quietness and in trust shall be your strength.

Isaiah 30:15

Blessed are those who trust in the LORD,
whose trust is the LORD.

Jeremiah 17:7

For we walk by faith, not by sight.

2 Corinthians 5:7

Now faith is the assurance of things hoped for, the conviction of things not seen.

Hebrews 11:1

Whenever you face trials of any kind, consider it nothing but joy, because you know that the testing of your faith produces endurance; and let endurance have its full effect, so that you may be mature and complete, lacking in nothing.

James 1:2-3

His divine power has given us everything needed for life and godliness, through the knowledge of him who called us by his own glory and goodness... For this very reason, you must make every effort to support your faith with goodness, and goodness with knowledge, and knowledge with self-control, and self-control with endurance, and endurance with godliness, and godliness with mutual affection, and mutual affection with love.

2 Peter 1:3-7

HOPE

5

HOPE

Be strong and take heart,
    all you who hope in the LORD.
        Psalm 31:24 NIV

May your unfailing love rest upon us, O LORD,
    even as we put our hope in you.
        Psalm 33:22 NIV

Why are you cast down, O my soul,
    and why are you disquieted within me?
Hope in God; for I shall again praise him,
    my help and my God.
        Psalm 42:11

Why are you cast down, O my soul,
    and why are you disquieted within me?
Hope in God; for I shall again praise him,
    my help and my God.
        Psalm 43:5

For God alone my soul waits in silence,
for my hope is from him.

Psalm 62:5

For you, O LORD, are my hope,
my trust, O LORD, from my youth.

Psalm 71:5

But I will hope continually,
and will praise you yet more and more.

Psalm 71:14

May those who sow in tears
reap with shouts of joy.

Psalm 125:5

I wait for the LORD, my soul waits,
and in his word I hope.

Psalm 130:5

Joyful are those…whose hope is in the LORD their God.

Psalm 146:5 NLT

Surely there is a future,
    and your hope will not be cut off.
Proverbs 23:18

O Lord, you are my God;
    I will exalt you and praise your name,
for in perfect faithfulness
    you have done marvelous things,
    things planned long ago.
Isaiah 25:1 NIV

"For I know the plans I have for you," declares the Lord, "plans to prosper you and not to harm you, plans to give you hope and a future."
Jeremiah 29:11 NIV

But this I call to mind, and therefore I have hope: The steadfast love of the Lord never ceases; his mercies never come to an end; they are new every morning; great is your faithfulness. "The Lord is my portion," says my soul, "therefore I will hope in him."
Lamentations 3:21-24 ESV

Very truly I tell you, you will weep and mourn while the world rejoices. You will grieve, but your grief will turn to joy.
John 16:20 NIV

And hope does not disappoint us, because God's love has been poured into our hearts through the Holy Spirit.

Romans 5:5

Now hope that is seen is not hope. For who hopes for what is seen? But if we hope for what we do not see, we wait for it with patience.

Romans 8:24-25

May the God of hope fill you with all joy and peace as you trust in him, so that you may overflow with hope by the power of the Holy Spirit.

Romans 15:13 NIV

Let us hold fast to the confession of our hope without wavering, for he who has promised is faithful.

Hebrews 10:23

LOVE

6

LOVE

Blessed be the Lord,
    for he has wondrously shown his steadfast love to
    me
    when I was beset as a city under siege.
I had said in my alarm,
    "I am driven far from your sight."
But you heard my supplications
    when I cried out to you for help.
Psalm 31:21-22

Your love, O Lord, reaches to the heavens,
    your faithfulness to the skies.
Psalm 36:5 NIV

How precious is your steadfast love, O God!
    All people may take refuge in the shadow of your
    wings.
Psalm 36:7

Give thanks to him, bless his name.
For the LORD is good;
his steadfast love endures forever,
and his faithfulness to all generations.
Psalm 100:4-5

I love the LORD, because he has heard
my voice and my supplications.
Because he inclined his ear to me,
therefore I will call on him as long as I live.
The snares of death encompassed me; . . .
I suffered distress and anguish.
Then I called on the name of the LORD:
"O LORD, I pray, save my life!"
Psalm 116:1-4

O give thanks to the LORD,
for he is good; his steadfast love endures forever!
Psalm 118:1

Let me hear of your steadfast love in the morning,
for in you I put my trust.
Teach me the way I should go,
for to you I lift up my soul.
Psalm 143:8

For the mountains may depart
    and the hills be removed,
but my steadfast love shall not depart from you,
    and my covenant of peace shall not be removed,
    says the LORD, who has compassion on you.

Isaiah 54:10

I have loved you with an everlasting love;
    therefore I have continued my faithfulness to you.

Jeremiah 31:3

The LORD your God is with you,
    he is mighty to save.
He will take great delight in you,
    he will quiet you with his love,
    he will rejoice over you with singing.

Zephaniah 3:17 NIV

Love knows no limit to its endurance, no end to its trust, no fading of its hope; it can outlast anything. It is, in fact, the one thing that still stands when all else has fallen.

1 Corinthians 13:7-8a JBP

And now faith, hope, and love abide, these three; and the greatest of these is love.

1 Corinthians 13:13

And, above everything else, be truly loving, for love is the golden chain of all the virtues.

Colossians 3:14 JBP

God is love.

1 John 4:16

There is no fear in love, but perfect love casts out fear; for fear has to do with punishment, and whoever fears has not reached perfection in love.

1 John 4:18

PEACE

7

PEACE

The Lord lift up his countenance upon you, and give you peace.

Numbers 6:26

Agree with God, and be at peace;
in this way good will come to you.

Job 22:21

By the tender mercy of our God,
the dawn from on high will break upon us,
to give light to those who sit in darkness and in the shadow of death,
to guide our feet into the way of peace.

Luke 1:78-79

"Peace I leave with you; my peace I give to you. I do not give to you as the world gives. Do not let your hearts be troubled, and do not let them be afraid."

John 14:27

You have made known to me the ways of life;
  you will make me full of gladness with your
  presence.

Acts 2:28

Do not worry about anything, but in everything by prayer and supplication with thanksgiving let your requests be made known to God. And the peace of God, which surpasses all understanding, will guard your hearts and your minds in Christ Jesus.

Philippians 4:6-7

Now may the LORD of peace himself give you peace at all times in all ways.

2 Thessalonians 3:16

May mercy, peace, and love be yours in abundance.

Jude 1:2

An Online Community of Grief Recovery
www.beyondthebrokenheart.com

Join the heart-healing community of grief recovery and support at BeyondTheBrokenHeart.com, where you can find resources of help and comfort gathered together for your use by author Julie Yarbrough. There you will find online forums, devotionals, a weekly blog, and help for finding or starting a grief support group in your congregation or community.

About the Author

Julie Yarbrough

Inspired by her personal experience after the death of her husband, Dr. Leighton Farrell, senior minister at Hyde Park United Methodist Church for many years, Julie established a grief-support group and began writing articles and books for persons who are grieving. She is president of Yarbrough Investments and lives in Dallas, Texas.